Going Batty
in Austin

by Mary Lindeen

Scott Foresman
is an imprint of

Glenview, Illinois • Boston, Massachusetts • Chandler, Arizona •
Upper Saddle River, New Jersey

Photographs

Every effort has been made to secure permission and provide appropriate credit for photographic material. The publisher deeply regrets any omission and pledges to correct errors called to its attention in subsequent editions.

Unless otherwise acknowledged, all photographs are the property of Pearson Education, Inc.

Photo locators denoted as follows: Top (T), Center (C), Bottom (B), Left (L), Right (R), Background (Bkgd)

Opener ©Steve Kaufman/CORBIS; **1** ©PirAli Photo/Graphic Studio; **3** ©Bill Heinsohn/Alamy; **4** ©Rex Curry/Alamy; **5** ©JTB Photo Communications, Inc./Alamy; **6** ©Radius Images/Jupiter Images; **7** ©Robert Sullivan/AFP/Getty Images; **8** Bob Daemmrich/PhotoEdit; **9** Robert Backman; **10** Robert Sullivan/AFP/Getty Images; **11** ©Map Resources/Alamy; **12** ©blickwinkel/Alamy; **13** ©blickwinkel/Alamy; **14** ©Peter Arnold, Inc./Alamy; **15** ©PirAli Photo/Graphic Studio; **16** ©Steve Kaufman/Corbis.

ISBN 13: 978-0-328-47267-3
ISBN 10:   0-328-47267-0

4 5 6 7 8 9 10 V010 13 12

It's a warm summer night in Austin, Texas. Hundreds of people are gathering near the Congress Avenue Bridge. What's everybody waiting for?

Bats!

Everyone is waiting to see bats! More than a million of them live under this bridge. When it gets dark, hungry bats fly out for dinner.

The Congress Avenue Bridge was built in 1980. The builders had no idea that Mexican free-tail bats would find homes under their bridge. These bats fly north from Mexico to have their babies and raise their young pups.

At first, people in Austin were afraid of the bats under the bridge. They thought the bats would attack them or make them sick.

6

Over time, people got to know more about the bats. They learned that bats are shy animals that fly at night. They learned that bats LOVE to eat insects! People weren't afraid anymore. They even began to celebrate this unusual bat colony.

The city of Austin has a celebration every summer called Batfest. People come to see a famous sculpture called *Nightwing*.

Even the city's hockey team joined in. The team is called the Ice Bats. Bats are everywhere in Austin!

Now people come to Austin just to see the bats fly out from under the bridge. Some people watch from the land. Others enjoy the event from small boats.

Austin's bat colony is one of the largest in North America. In the summertime, bats actually outnumber people in Austin!

There are a lot of bats flying around Austin at dusk. Why don't they bump into each other, or into people? Bats are excellent night fliers.

Bats use echolocation when they fly. They make high-pitched calls out of their mouths or noses. The calls bounce, or echo, off nearby objects. A bat listens for echoes with its big ears. The echoes tell where things are and how big those things are.

The bats are great for Austin. They eat tons of insects every year. One bat can eat 600 mosquitoes in an hour!

Lots of tourists come to Austin every year to see the bats. They spend millions of dollars on hotel rooms, food, and bat toys.

At first, the people of Austin worried that their town was going batty. But now they know that it's good to be the "Bat Capital of America."